D0602061

Grizzlies
and Other Bears

Concept and Product Development: Editorial Options, Inc.
Series Designer: Karen Donica
Book Author: Shirley A. Petersen

For information on other World Book products, visit us at our Web site at http://www.worldbook.com

For information on sales to schools and libraries in the United States, call 1-800-975-3250.

For information on sales to schools and libraries in Canada, call 1-800-837-5365.

World Book, Inc.
233 N. Michigan Avenue
Chicago, IL 60601

Library of Congress Cataloging-in-Publication Data

Grizzlies and other bears.
p. cm. -- (World Book's animals of the world)
ISBN 0-7166-1212-7 -- ISBN 0-7166-1211-9 (set)
1. Grizzly bear--Juvenile literature. 2. Bears--Juvenile literature. [1. Grizzly bear. 2. Bears.] World Book, Inc. II. Series.

QL737.C27 G7435 2001
599.784--dc21 2001017526

Printed in Singapore

1 2 3 4 5 6 7 8 9 05 04 03 02 01

World Book's Animals of the World

Grizzlies
and Other Bears

World Book, Inc.
A Scott Fetzer Company
Chicago

Contents

Why am I the bamboo bear?

Bear hug, anyone?

What Is a Bear?

The powerful grizzly you see here is just one kind of bear. Bears are mammals. They have fur on their bodies, and mother bears use their own milk to nurse their young.

Bears belong to an order of animals called carnivores *(KAHR nuh vawrz).* Carnivores are animals that eat meat. Like other carnivores (such as wolves), bears have sharp canine teeth. They use these teeth to tear meat apart. Bears, however, don't eat just meat. They also feed on plants.

Grizzlies belong to a species called big brown bears. Other species include American black bears, Asiatic black bears, polar bears, sun bears, sloth bears, and spectacled bears. Some scientists also classify pandas as bears.

Grizzly bear

Where in the World Do Bears Live?

The map shows where in the world bears can now be found in the wild. Most of them live north of the equator.

North America is home to grizzlies and other big brown bears. But the most common North American bears are American black bears.

There are big brown bears in Europe and Asia, too. Asiatic black bears live in Asia, as you might expect. Asia is also home to sloth bears and sun bears.

Polar bears live on the ice fields of the Arctic. This is the region around the North Pole.

The only kind of bear that lives in South America is the spectacled bear. No wild bears live in Africa, Australia, or Antarctica.

World Map

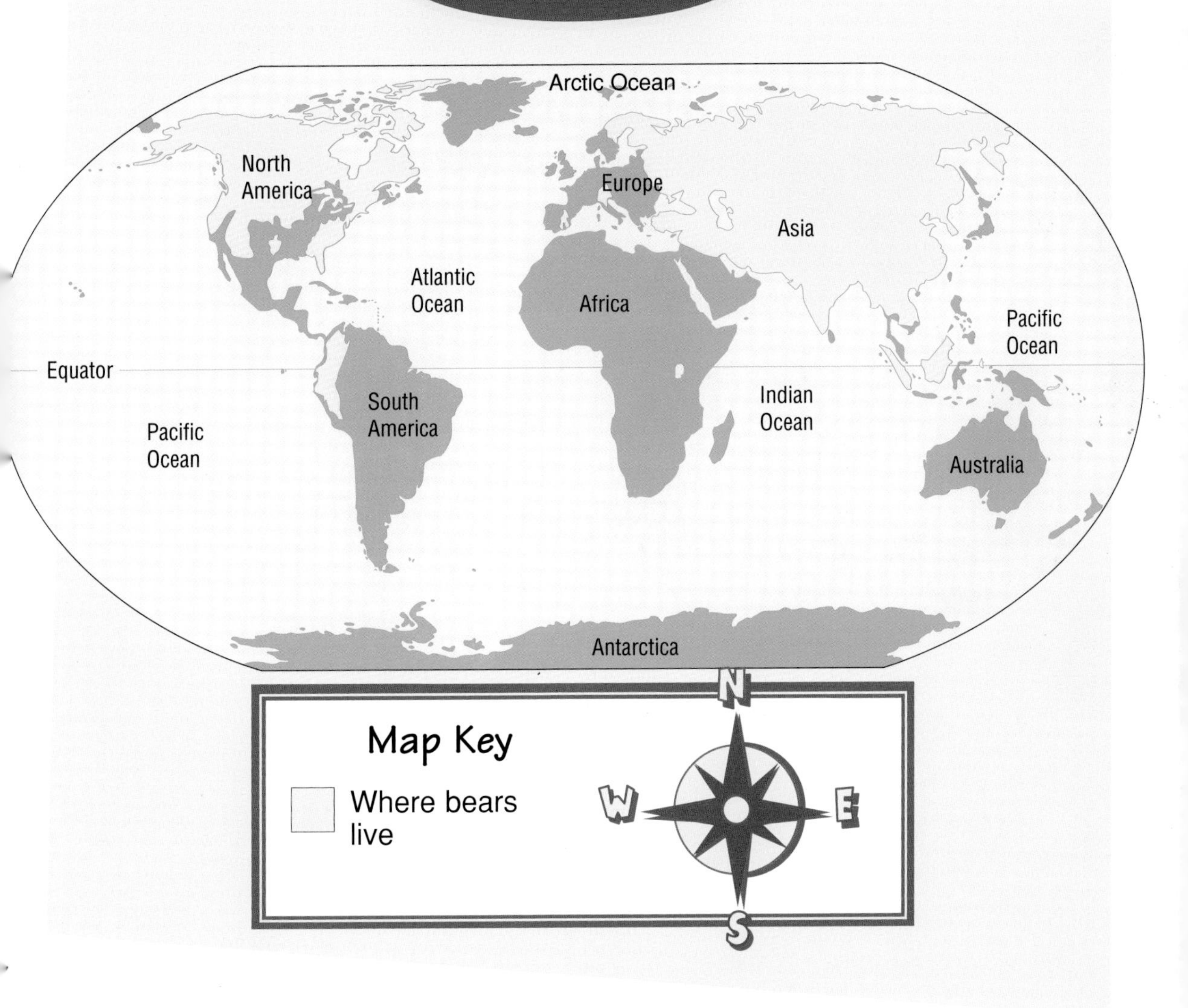
Arctic Ocean
North America
Europe
Asia
Atlantic Ocean
Africa
Pacific Ocean
Equator
South America
Indian Ocean
Pacific Ocean
Australia
Antarctica
N
Map Key
Where bears live
W
E
S

What's So Grizzly About Grizzly Bears?

Grizzly bears are grizzled, which means "streaked with gray." A grizzly's underfur—the fur closest to its skin—is shaggy and mostly shades of brown. But the grizzly also has outer hairs that are white or silver-tipped. This gives the bears a "grizzly" look.

Grizzlies are big brown bears, but don't let the word *brown* fool you. Although grizzlies are usually dark brown, they may be cream to almost black in color.

Most adult grizzlies can grow to 8 feet (2.4 meters) long. If one stood on its hind legs in your living room, it might hit its head on the ceiling! A male grizzly may weigh up to 500 pounds (230 kilograms)—the weight of two very large men. Female grizzlies usually weigh 350 to 400 pounds (160 to 180 kilograms). Even though they are smaller than males, female grizzlies are just as fierce—especially when protecting their young.

Grizzly bear

What's Under All That Fur?

Very strong bones and powerful muscles are under that mass of fur. Here you see the skeleton of a grizzly. A grizzly's skeleton is much like that of other bears.

Bears have large heads and skulls. They have powerful jaws. They have broad shoulders. A grizzly also has a hump of muscle on its shoulders. So do other big brown bears. One way to tell a big brown bear from other kinds of bears is to look for this hump.

Like other bears, a grizzly has four short legs. Just two of them can support the bear's entire weight when it stands.

A grizzly has broad, flat paws. There are five toes on each paw. The toes have long, sharp claws that do not pull back, or retract. While most other animals walk on their tiptoes, bears walk on the soles of their feet—just as people do.

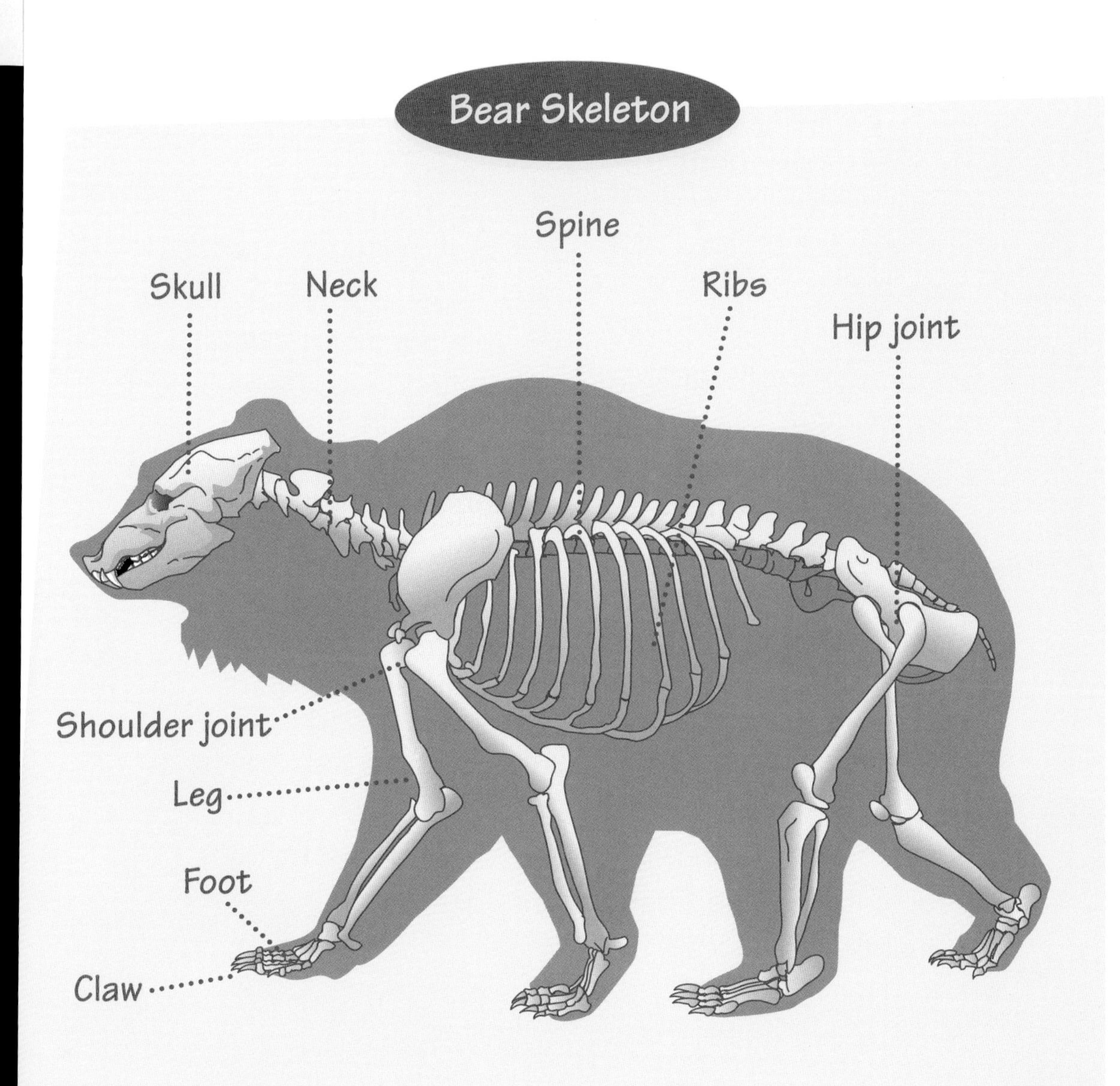
Bear Skeleton
Spine
Skull
Neck
Ribs
Hip joint
Shoulder joint
Leg
Foot
Claw

...arpest Sense?

Take a good look at this grizzly's head. The bear's eyes and ears are small for such a big animal. But the bear's snout and nose are quite large. Grizzlies depend on their sense of smell to find food. Smell is a bear's sharpest sense.

A grizzly bear can smell carrion *(KAIR ee uhn),* or the flesh of a dead animal, from very far away. How far away? Some scientists say that bears can smell carrion from 18 miles (29 kilometers) away. That's some sense of smell!

Grizzlies are out and about during the day and at night. They seem to be most active at dusk or at dawn, however. And, in places where there are people, these bears tend to be nocturnal, or active at night.

Grizzly bear

What's for Dinner?

Grizzly bears do eat meat. They eat land animals, such as elk and moose, as well as fish. But grizzlies also feed on plants. The grizzly you see here is searching for berries. These animals also eat grasses, leaves, and roots.

It takes a lot of food to fuel a grizzly bear's body. For this reason, the bears spend most of their time foraging, or searching for food.

In summer and early fall, a grizzly may eat 80 to 90 pounds (36 to 41 kilograms) of food a day. You would have to have about 300 hamburgers a day to keep up with the bear. Later in the fall, the bear stuffs itself even more. It may gain several pounds of fat a day. The extra fat helps the bear survive the long winter, when it may eat nothing for months.

Grizzly bear foraging

How Do Grizzlies Survive the Winter?

Many animals hibernate *(HY buhr nayt)* during the winter. During hibernation, animals go into a deep sleep. Grizzlies do go into a winter sleep—but some scientists say it is not true hibernation. During winter sleep, a grizzly can rouse itself right away if it needs to. This is especially important for female bears that may be caring for cubs.

Some grizzlies find caves or other natural shelters for their winter sleep. Others dig dens. They start digging in the fall, before the ground freezes. Often they dig into steep slopes. A den entrance is usually very narrow, but then it widens into a larger sleeping room.

Grizzly bears usually move into their winter homes between October and December. At that time of year, the plants that bears usually eat have disappeared.

Grizzly in den

When Is a Grizzly Bear Bare?

A grizzly looks bare—or hairless—when it is first born. But that changes quickly. The cubs you see are just 10 days old, and they already have some fur.

The mother grizzly usually gives birth to two cubs, but she may have one to four. The cubs' eyes are closed at first. They stay closed for about a month. The mother bear cuddles her cubs to keep them warm and safe.

Grizzly cubs are quite tiny at birth. They usually weigh 12 to 24 ounces (340 to 680 grams). That's about the size of a small gray squirrel. But the cubs grow quickly as they feed on their mother's milk. This milk is very rich in fat—many times richer than a human mother's milk.

Most grizzlies leave their winter dens between March and May. Mothers with new cubs, however, usually stay in their dens longer than bears without cubs. Cubs are frisky and playful when they come out of the den.

Newborn grizzlies

How Do Grizzly Cubs Learn?

Grizzly cubs need to learn certain skills in order to survive on their own. Until then, they depend on their mother. The mother bear feeds and protects her young. If a mother grizzly dies, her cubs are likely to die also.

Cubs learn how to forage from their mother. She also teaches them how to fish. Cubs may continue to use the mother's fishing method even after they grow up.

The cubs also learn through play. They practice chasing and stalking each other. They chew, swat, and jaw wrestle. These activities build muscles.

Grizzly cubs usually stay with their mother for the first $1\frac{1}{2}$ to $3\frac{1}{2}$ years of their lives. Then the family drifts apart. The young adults may den where their mother denned for another year or two. But then they go off on their own.

Grizzly mother teaching cubs

When Do Grizzlies Get Together?

Grizzlies are loners. They live alone. They hunt alone. They feed alone. But once a year, they do have a kind of get-together. That time comes in the summer, when the streams are filled with salmon. Salmon and other fish are an important part of a grizzly's diet.

Grizzlies use different methods to catch fish. Some grizzlies stand still in the water. They watch the fish closely. When a fish jumps out of the water, the grizzly snatches it with its jaws. Other grizzlies swat the fish out of the water and up onto the shore.

Some grizzlies dive or "snorkel" under the water in order to find fish. Sometimes a bear launches itself onto the salmon in a bellyflop.

Grizzlies fishing

How Do Grizzlies Communicate?

Grizzlies don't communicate much. Or, if they do, we don't know a lot about how they do it. But scientists think that these bears do signal each other.

One way that a grizzly signals another bear is by showing off its size. A small bear will usually run from a bigger bear. Two bears that are the same size may circle each other. Perhaps they are trying to figure out which is stronger!

An angry grizzly will signal by lowering its head and flattening its ears. The bear may even growl or snort.

Some grizzlies stretch up tall and use their claws to scratch the bark of trees. This leaves behind the grizzly's scent. Its scent lets other bears know that the grizzly is around. This may keep grizzlies from running into each other and probably prevents fights.

Grizzly bear

Which Brown Bears Are Bigger Than Grizzlies?

Like grizzlies, Kodiaks are big brown bears. But Kodiaks are even bigger than grizzlies. A Kodiak can stand 9 to 10 feet (2.7 to 3.0 meters) tall. In the fall, a Kodiak can weigh around 1,500 pounds (680 kilograms).

Like their grizzly cousins, Kodiaks love salmon. And there are many salmon where the bears live—on and around Kodiak Island. Kodiak Island, which is off the coast of Alaska, is a salmon spawning ground. A spawning ground is a place where fish lay eggs and breed. It's also a great place for bears to find their favorite foods.

Kodiaks are excellent fishers. A mother can catch 15 salmon in an hour to feed herself and her cubs. Kodiaks also feed on beached whales.

Kodiak bear

Do Polar Bears Live at the North Pole?

Polar bears don't live at the North Pole. But they do live in the Arctic region around the North Pole. Polar bears do not live anywhere near the South Pole. And despite what you might think, polar bears are never found in the same habitat as penguins.

Fully grown male polar bears are around 8 to 11 feet (2.4 to 3.4 meters) long. Some weigh more than 1,000 pounds (454 kilograms). Females are smaller than males.

Polar bears differ from other bears in their coloring. Polar bears are white, creamy, or yellowish-white. This coloring helps these bears blend in with the snowy-white of their habitat. It hides, or camouflages *(KAM uh fluh zhuhz),* them while they hunt.

Polar bears eat mostly meat. They prey on sea animals, such as fish, seals, walrus, and dead whales. Polar bears also eat berries and grasses—when they can find them.

Polar bear

How Do Polar Bears Get Around?

Polar bears get around easily in and out of water. That's important because polar bears live where there is a lot of sea ice. The sea ice breaks apart during the summer. The broken off pieces are called ice floes.

Polar bears travel on these floes and swim between them, islands, and the mainland. Polar bears are the best swimmers of all bears. They can swim at speeds of 3 to 6 miles (5 to 10 kilometers) an hour. A polar bear's large forepaws act like paddles to move the animal through water. Webbing between the toes also helps the bear swim. Its long neck keeps the bear's head above water.

On land, the polar bear's broad paws spread weight and act like snowshoes. This helps the bear run fast. A polar bear can run up to 35 miles (56.3 kilometers) an hour—fast enough to catch reindeer.

Polar bear on ice floe

How Do Polar Bears Keep Warm?

Polar bears have thick layers of fat beneath their skin. This fat helps keep them warm. The bears also have warm fur coats.

A polar bear's fur has an undercoat and an overcoat. The undercoat is made up of fine, white hairs. These provide warmth. The overcoat is made up of long guard hairs that shed water easily. The guard hairs are hollow. This helps trap heat from the sun, providing more warmth. When they get wet, the guard hairs mat together. This helps keep the bear's skin dry. And a polar bear's skin is black, which helps keep in heat.

Polar bears have fur on their paws. This keeps their feet warm. It also prevents them from slipping on the ice.

Polar bear

How Do Polar Bears Hunt?

Like other bears, polar bears rely on their sense of smell to find prey. On land, they follow their prey on foot. Then they ambush, or attack by surprise.

A polar bear's favorite prey is the ringed seal. A bear might spot a seal on an ice floe. The polar bear swims forward slowly toward the floe. Only its head is above water. Then the bear jumps up onto the ice and pounces on the seal.

Other times, a polar bear sits next to a seal's breathing hole in the ice. It waits for a seal to come up for air. When it does, the bear grabs the seal with powerful forepaws and claws. It drags the seal up onto the ice and then eats it. A polar bear may share its kill with other bears. It would rather do this than fight to keep the meal to itself.

Polar bear at seal hole

Are American Black Bears Always Black?

Believe it or not, American black bears are not always black. In fact, they come in many different colors. Some have black coats, brown noses, and white patches on their chests. Others are rusty brown. They are known as cinnamon black bears.

Then there are Kermode's *(KUR mohdz)* bears. These American black bears are often creamy-white, but sometimes they are pure white. They even have white claws.

The rarest American black bear is the glacier bear. It has a mix of gray and black hairs. This mix makes the bear look blue.

American black bears are smaller and lighter than grizzlies. An American black bear is about 5 feet (1.5 meters) long and weighs 200 to 300 pounds (91 to 140 kilograms). These bears are great tree-climbers. In fact, climbing trees is one way they avoid danger.

American black bear

What Is a Moon Bear?

The Asiatic black bear is sometimes called a moon bear. Look at the marking on this bear's chest. It looks like a crescent moon, doesn't it? This bear also has fur of a lighter color on its lower lip and chin.

Asiatic black bears are about the same size as American black bears. But the Asiatic black bears have shiny black fur. They also have thick manes around their faces. A mane may grow to be 6 inches (15 centimeters) long.

Asiatic black bears hunt large and small mammals, including farm animals. They also eat ants and other insects, fruits, nuts, and berries.

Asiatic black bear

How Are American and Asiatic Black Bears Alike?

Both American and Asiatic black bears climb very well. Their claws are strong and short—only about 1 to 2 inches (2.5 to 5 centimeters) long. The claws are also sharply curved. This helps the bears climb trees with ease.

Trees are important to both kinds of black bears. Mothers often send their cubs up trees to protect them. Sometimes Asiatic black bears make day beds in trees. They rest in the trees during the day and come down to feed at night.

Both American and some Asiatic black bears go into a winter sleep when the weather gets cold. They do this because food is hard to find then. Other Asiatic black bears that live in warm climates do not sleep through the winter. They never run out of food.

Asiatic black bear

Which Bear Got a Name Change?

The sloth bear looks a lot like the slow-moving, tree-dwelling animal called a sloth. In fact, it looks so much like the sloth that scientists in the late 1700's called it a "bearlike sloth." After further study, the scientists realized their mistake and named it "sloth bear."

Like all bears, a sloth bear has a heavy body and rounded ears. Its tail is short, but it is longer than that of many bears. A sloth bear has long black fur and a light-colored patch on its chest.

Sloth bears are more social than other bears. They communicate with facial expressions and a variety of sounds. Sloth bears roar, howl, squeal, yelp, huff, rattle, and gurgle. Mothers often carry cubs on their backs (just as sloths do) until the babies are quite large.

Sloth bear

Are Sloth Bears Lazy?

Sloth bears move with a low, shuffling walk. This makes them look lazy. But, when they are alarmed, they can gallop faster than a person can run.

Sloth bears are not at all lazy when it comes to finding food. They work hard to find it. Their big feet and long, curved claws make them good diggers. Sloth bears have no incisors, or front teeth, and the roofs of their mouths are hollowed out. This creates a vacuum effect that helps the sloth bear suck up its favorite food—termites!

Sloth bears dig into hard, tall termite pillars. A sloth bear inserts its snout, blows away the dust, and sucks the insects into its mouth. The sucking noise is so loud that it can be heard 200 yards (183 meters) away!

Sloth bear

Do Spectacled Bears Wear Spectacles?

No, spectacled bears do not wear spectacles, or eyeglasses. But these bears do have white or tan markings around their eyes. These markings make the bears look as if they are wearing glasses.

A spectacled bear's markings are as special as a person's fingerprints. No two bears have the same markings!

The spectacled bear has the same shaggy coat and heavy body that most bears have. But it has white markings on its neck and chest. Like other bears, the spectacled bear has a short tail and rounded ears.

Spectacled bear

Where Do Spectacled Bears Find Food?

Like most bears, the spectacled bear likes honey. But it also likes its veggies. It feeds mostly on such things as corn, palm leaves, cactus, and sugar cane, as well as fruits and nuts. This bear has very strong jaws, so it can chew things that other animals may not want to bother with.

Spectacled bears find much of their food in trees. They use their sharp claws to climb trees. Often the bears move from tree to tree as fruits ripen. They may spend three or four days eating the fruit of one tree before moving on to the next.

Spectacled bears raid farmers' crops and attack their beehives. Farmers don't like these bears! But spectacled bears are important to the forests in which they live. They scatter the seeds of trees and other plants.

Spectacled bear

Which Bears Are the Smallest?

The smallest bears are sun bears. A sun bear is only about 3 feet (0.9 meter) long and weighs 60 to 100 pounds (27 to 45 kilograms). That's the size of a large dog.

Sun bears are different from other bears in many ways. Their fur is black and short, not shaggy like that of most bears. Sun bears have solid, sleek bodies. Their noses may be gray or orange. The sun bear also has a white or yellow marking on its chest. Long ago, people believed the marking looked like a rising sun—thus the name sun bear.

Sun bears mostly search for food at night. They rest during the day. To protect themselves from predators, sun bears climb trees. They build nestlike beds in the trees.

Sun bear

How Do Bears Size Up?

Although bears have similar shapes, they come in very different sizes. The largest bear of all is the Kodiak, an Alaskan brown bear. Next comes the polar bear. In fact, some polar bears have longer bodies than Kodiaks do—although they don't weigh quite so much. Other big brown bears, such as the grizzly, rank third in terms of size.

As the chart shows, some kinds of bears are fairly close in size. Spectacled bears, American black bears, sloth bears, and Asiatic black bears are all about the same length. Spectacled bears weigh more than the other three species of bears, however. Sloth bears weigh less than the other three. The smallest of all the bears are the sun bears.

Within each group of bears, some members are bigger than others. Males in a group are usually bigger than females.

Comparison Chart

Alaskan brown bear

American black bear

Polar bear

Asiatic black bear

Grizzly bear

Sloth bear

Spectacled bear

Sun bear

How Does the Giant Panda Fit In?

A giant panda is often called a panda bear. But not all scientists agree that it belongs in the bear family.

At one time, the giant panda and a similar animal, the red panda, were placed in the raccoon family. Pandas share many traits with raccoons. For one thing, they have similar markings. They also use their front paws to grasp food. It's easy to see why scientists grouped these animals together.

Now, however, scientists tell a lot about an animal by studying its genes. Genes are tiny items found within an animal's cells. But genes have a big job. They decide such traits as fur color, body size, and eye color of an animal. Many scientists think giant pandas and bears have similar genes. They say that giant pandas belong in the bear family.

Other scientists think giant and red pandas are so closely related to each other that they should be placed in their own family—the panda family!

Giant panda

Are Giant Pandas Picky Eaters?

Yes! Giant pandas rarely eat anything but plants. And they eat mainly one kind of plant. They feed on bamboo shoots, stems, and leaves found in the bamboo forests of China.

Compared to most bears, giant pandas are actually quite small. They weigh around 200 to 300 pounds (90 to 140 kilograms). But they eat a lot for their size. Giant pandas eat up to 85 pounds (39 kilograms) of bamboo every day. Giant pandas have back teeth that are very wide and flat. These teeth help the panda grind all that bamboo.

China once had a lot of bamboo. But the bamboo forests are disappearing fast. Giant pandas are losing their homes and food supply. That's why these animals are endangered. There are probably fewer than 1,000 left in the wild. China now has laws to protect giant pandas.

Giant panda

Are Bears in Danger?

Bears will survive only if they have habitats in which to live. Grizzlies, for example, used to roam over large parts of North America. Now they live mostly in western Canada and Alaska. Sloth bears, sun bears, and spectacled bears are also losing their forest homes.

But there is good news for some bears—polar bears. So many of these bears had been hunted that people got worried. In 1973, five countries where polar bears live signed an agreement. As a result, polar bears are now protected by law.

There is hope for other bears, too. Conservationists are setting aside land so that these wild creatures have places to live. Many zoos now have bear-breeding programs for endangered animals. Zoos all over the world are beginning to work together to help preserve these magnificent animals.

Grizzly bears
on the alert

Bear Fun Facts

- The phrase "licked into shape" comes from an old belief that bears were born so soft and shapeless that their mothers had to lick them into the shape of a bear.
- Brown bears and polar bears are so closely related that they can mate and produce offspring.
- In many zoos, bears do not go into a winter sleep because their cages and enclosures are too warm.
- Sloth bears like honey so much that they are sometimes called honey bears.
- When polar bears are close to prey, they lie flat on the ground. That way they don't cast shadows that might scare off the prey.
- The record-holding adult male polar bear weighed in at 2,210 pounds (1,002 kilograms). It was over 11 feet (3.4 meters) long.
- If you live in the Northern Hemisphere, you can see bears in the nighttime sky. These bears are the constellations Ursa Major (Great Bear) and Ursa Minor (Little Bear).

Glossary

canine teeth Long, sharp teeth.

carnivore An animal that eats mostly meat.

carrion Dead or decaying flesh or meat that is not fit to be eaten by people.

claw A sharp, hooked nail on an animal's foot.

endangered In danger of becoming extinct.

floe A mass or sheet of floating ice.

forage To search for food.

forepaws Front paws.

gene A tiny part of a cell of an animal. Genes determine the characteristics that offspring inherit from their parents.

glacier A large mass of ice in very cold regions. A glacier is formed by snow that does not melt.

habitat The area where an animal lives.

hibernate To spend the winter in a deep sleep, during which the body temperature drops and breathing slows down.

mammal A warm-blooded animal that feeds its young on the mother's milk.

nocturnal Active at night.

order A group of animals or plants that are similar in many ways.

predator An animal that eats other animals.

prey Any animal that is hunted for food by another animal.

prey on To feed by seizing prey.

skeleton A framework of bones that supports and protects the body of an animal.

species A group of the same kinds of animals.

termite An insect that feeds on wood.

territory A place that animals keep for themselves only.

underfur The fur closest to an animal's skin.

Index

(**Boldface** indicates a photo, map, or illustration.)

Picture Acknowledgments: Front & Back Cover: © John Shaw, Bruce Coleman Inc.; © Erwin & Peggy Bauer, Bruce Coleman Collection; © Tom Brakefield, Bruce Coleman Inc.; © Tim Davis, Photo Researchers; © Eckart Pott, Bruce Coleman Collection

© Erwin & Peggy Bauer, Bruce Coleman Inc. 17; © Erwin & Peggy Bauer, Bruce Coleman Collection 11; © Tom Brakefield, Bruce Coleman Inc. 4, 57, 59; © Joe Coleman, Bruce Coleman Inc. 53; © Tim Davis, Photo Researchers 15, 39; © D. Robert Franz, Bruce Coleman Inc. 31; © Dan Guravich, Photo Researchers 35; © Zig Leszczynski, Animals Animals 45; © Tom McHugh, Photo Researchers 5, 27, 29; © Michael McKavett, Bruce Coleman Collection 47; © Mark Moffett, Minden Pictures 51; © Mark Newman, Bruce Coleman Inc. 61; © Mark Newman, Photo Researchers 41; © Eckart Pott, Bruce Coleman Collection 37; © D. Puleston, Photo Researchers 33; © Hans Reinhard, Bruce Coleman Collection 25; © Leonard Lee Rue, Bruce Coleman Collection 21; © John Shaw, Bruce Coleman Inc. 3, 7; © Stouffer Productions from Animals Animals 19; © David Welling, Animals Animals 49; Terry Whitaker, Photo Researchers 43; © Art Wolfe, Photo Researchers 23.

Illustrations: WORLD BOOK illustration by Michael DiGiorgio 13, 55; WORLD BOOK illustration by Karen Donica 9, 62.

Bear Classification

Scientists classify animals by placing them into groups. The animal kingdom is a group that contains all the world's animals. Phylum, class, order, and family are smaller groups. Each phylum contains many classes. A class contains orders, and a family contains individual species. Each species also has its own scientific name. Here is how the animals in this book fit in to this system.

Animals with backbones and their relatives (Phylum Chordata)

Mammals (Class Mammalia)

Carnivores (Order Carnivora)

Bears (Family Ursidae)

American black bear. . . . . *Ursus americanus*
Asiatic black bear . . . . *Ursus thibetanus*
Brown bear (includes grizzly and kodiak). . . . . *Ursus arctos*
Giant panda . . . . *Aluropoda melanoleuca*
Polar bear. . . . . *Ursus maritimus*
Sloth bear. . . . . *Melursus ursinus*
Spectacled bear. . . . . *Tremarctos ornatus*
Sun bear. . . . . *Helarctos malayanus*

Raccoon, red panda, and their relatives (Family Procyonidae)

Red panda . . . . *Ailurus fulgens*